Contents

Any words appearing in the text in bold, **like this**, are explained in the Glossary.

Introducing arthropods

Arthropods are **invertebrates**. This means they do not have internal bony **skeletons** and they do not have a backbone. Three out of four of all known animal **species** are arthropods. Over a million species of living and **fossil** arthropods have been described and named. They are found in all climates, and a wide range of habitats from oceans to high mountains.

Chewers and non-chewers

Most scientists divide the phylum Arthropoda into two major groups or sub-phyla – Mandibulata and Chelicerata – depending on the shape of their mouthparts and whether or not they have sensory feelers called **antennae**.

Arthropods with chewing mouthparts, called **mandibles**, and one or two pairs of antennae are classified as mandibulates. This large group includes hexapods (insects and other six-legged arthropods), myriapods (centipedes and millipedes) and crustaceans (water fleas, crabs and lobsters). Some scientists think that the mandibulates should be further divided into two groups – crustaceans and uniramians – to separate crabs and lobsters from insects and myriapods.

Chelicerates have pincer-like **appendages** on the head and do not have antennae. This group includes arachnids (spiders, mites and ticks), sea spiders and horseshoe crabs.

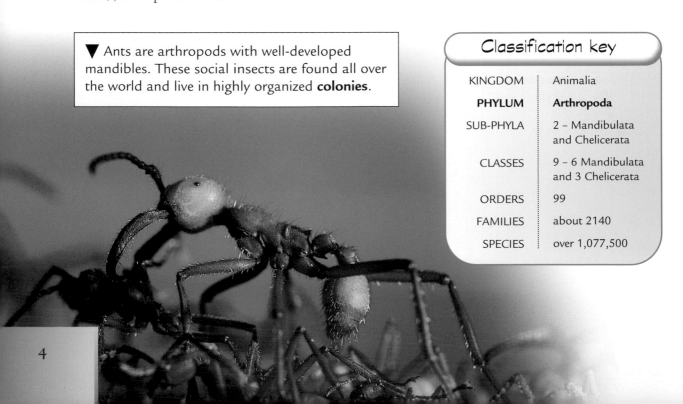

▼ Ants are arthropods with well-developed mandibles. These social insects are found all over the world and live in highly organized **colonies**.

Classification key

KINGDOM	Animalia
PHYLUM	**Arthropoda**
SUB-PHYLA	2 – Mandibulata and Chelicerata
CLASSES	9 – 6 Mandibulata and 3 Chelicerata
ORDERS	99
FAMILIES	about 2140
SPECIES	over 1,077,500

Arthropods

Ruth Miller

www.raintreepublishers.co.uk

Visit our website to find out more information about **Raintree** books.

To order:
☎ Phone 44 (0) 1865 888113
▤ Send a fax to 44 (0) 1865 314091
💻 Visit the Raintree Bookshop at **www.raintreepublishers.co.uk** to browse our catalogue and order online.

Produced for Raintree by
White-Thomson Publishing Ltd
Bridgewater Business Centre, 210 High Street,
Lewes, East Sussex, BN7 2NH

First published in Great Britain by
Raintree, Halley Court, Jordan Hill, Oxford OX2 8EJ,
part of Harcourt Education.
Raintree is a registered trademark of Harcourt Education Ltd.

© Harcourt Education Ltd 2005
First published in paperback in 2006
The moral right of the proprietor has been asserted.

Consultant: Dr Rod Preston-Mafham
Editorial: Katie Orchard, Nick Hunter and Catherine Clarke
Design: Tim Mayer
Picture Research: Morgan Interactive Ltd
Production: Amanda Meaden

Originated by Dot Gradations Ltd
Printed in China by WKT Company Limited

ISBN 1 844 43772 8 (hardback) ISBN 1 844 43782 5 (paperback)
09 08 07 06 05   10 09 08 07 06
10 9 8 7 6 5 4 3 2 1   10 9 8 7 6 5 4 3 2 1

British Library Cataloguing in Publication Data
Miller, Ruth
Arthropods. - (Animal Kingdom)
595
A full catalogue record for this book is available from
the British Library

Acknowledgements
The publishers would like to thank the following for permission
to reproduce photographs: Corbis p.35 top; Digital Vision Title
page, pp. 4, 6, 8, 18 bottom, 19, 24 top, 28 top, 29 top, 48
bottom, 53 bottom, 58, 60, 61; Ecoscene pp. 11 top (Chinch
Gryniewicz), 15 top (Wayne Lawler), 17 top (Fritz Pölking), 21
top, 24 bottom (Kjell Sandved), 27 bottom (Robin Williams),
29 (Chinch Gryniewicz), 33 top (Jeff Collett), 50-51 (Martin
Lillicrap), 55 top (Erik Schaffer), 55 bottom (Chinch
Gryniewicz), 56 (Tom Ennis), 57 top (Chinch Gryniewicz);
Ecoscene-Papilio pp. 10 (Lando Pescatori), 11 bottom (William
Dunn), 12 top (Lando Pescatori), 14 and 16 (Robert Pickett),
18 top (Alastair Shay), 22 (Lando Pescatori), 23 top, 31 top
(Robert Pickett), 40, 41 top, 42 bottom, 54 (Robert Pickett);
Nature PL pp. 34, 35 bottom (Jurgen Freund), 36 (Chris
Packham), 48 top (Bernard Castelein), 53 top (John Cancalosi);
NHPA pp. 5 top (Daniel Heuclin), 7 top (James Carmichael), 9
top, 13 (Stephen Dalton), 15 bottom (Nigel Callow), 16-17
(Stephen Dalton), 21 bottom (Anthony Bannister), 23 bottom
(Pete Oxford), 25 (Stephen Dalton), 26 (Eric Solder), 27 top
(John Shaw), 31 bottom (Nigel Callow), 32 top (Yves Lanceau),
37 top (B Jones and M Shimlock), 37 bottom (Anthony
Bannister), 38 (G.I. Bernard), 39 top (Anthony Bannister), 41
bottom (B Jones and M Shimlock), 43 top, 45 bottom (Daniel
Heuclin), 46 top (Peter Parks), 46 bottom (Anthony Bannister),
47 (Daniel Heuclin), 49 top (Stephen Dalton), 50 left (ANT), 51
right (James Carmichael), 52 (Daniel Heuclin), 57 bottom
(Stephen Dalton); Photodisc Contents page, 5 bottom, 7 bottom,
9 bottom, 30, 33 bottom, 44, 45 top, 59; Premaphotos Wildlife
pp. 20, 39, 43 bottom (Preston-Mafham).

Front cover photograph of Sally Lightfoot crabs reproduced with
permission of Corbis (martin Harvey/Gallo Images).
Back cover photograph of a honey bee reproduced with
permission of Digital Vision.

Classification

Living **organisms** are classified, or organized, according to how closely related one organism is to another. The basic group in classification is the species, for example humans belong to the species *Homo sapiens*. A species is a group of individuals that are similar to each other and that can **interbreed** with one another. Species are grouped together into genera (singular: genus). A genus may contain a number of species that share some features. *Homo* is the human genus. Genera are grouped together in families, the families grouped into orders and the orders grouped into classes. Classes are grouped together in phyla (singular: phylum) and finally the phyla are grouped into kingdoms. Kingdoms are the largest groups. Arthropods belong to the animal kingdom. (To find out more see pages 58–59.)

▲ Most species of fiddler crabs live in the mud of mangrove swamps in **tropical** climates. They have long, stalked eyes and the males have one enormous claw, which they waggle to attract females and to warn off any rival males.

◄ Tarantulas are the largest spiders, with bodies that may grow to a width of 12 centimetres and a leg span of up to 28 centimetres.

Arthropod features

Arthropods have segmented bodies with jointed legs. The body is covered on the outside with a tough, flexible layer called the **cuticle**. This layer forms an outer **skeleton**, or **exoskeleton**. Other animals, such as mammals and birds, have a bony skeleton inside the body, called an endoskeleton. In most groups of arthropods, the body has three distinct parts – the head, the **thorax** and the **abdomen**. The bodies of most arthropods are clearly divided into a number of segments, or compartments. The head contains the brain. It is made up of six segments, but the segments are not so clearly defined as in the thorax and the abdomen. The head has paired mouthparts, for feeding, and sense organs such as eyes.

Jointed legs

The most **characteristic** feature of the arthropods is their **appendages** (jointed structures attached to the body segments). The appendages on the head are **adapted** to help in feeding, while those on the rest of the body are usually adapted for walking or swimming and are often referred to as 'legs'. In some arthropods, appendages on the abdomen may be adapted for reproduction.

▼ Scorpions show characteristic arthropod features. They are easily recognized by their large claw-like **pedipalps** and their curved tail.

▼ Wood borers are beetles that live in dead wood. Their mouthparts are adapted to making tunnels through the timber.

Exoskeleton

An important feature of arthropods is their hard, rigid exoskeleton. It provides support for **locomotion** (getting from one place to another) and protection from enemies. It also prevents the body organs from being damaged or losing too much water. This type of skeleton has to be shed to allow for growth. All arthropods undergo **moulting**, or shedding, of the cuticle. During the time that the new exoskeleton, or cuticle, is hardening, the animal can increase in size.

Respiration

In most arthropods that live on land, such as insects, gas exchange for **respiration** takes place through a system of air-filled tubes, called **tracheae**. These transport air from the atmosphere directly to the body tissues. They open to the outside of the body through a series of tiny **pores**, or **spiracles**, in the cuticle. Most **aquatic** arthropods (those that live in water such as crabs and lobsters) breathe using **gills**.

▼ The phylum Arthropoda includes a wide range of very different-looking animals. However, there are some shared characteristics.

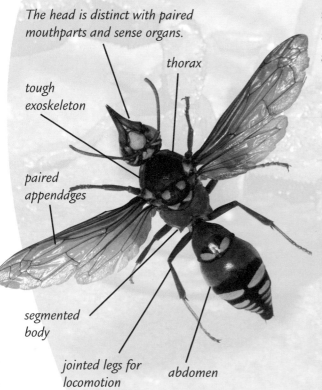

The head is distinct with paired mouthparts and sense organs.

thorax

tough exoskeleton

paired appendages

segmented body

jointed legs for locomotion

abdomen

Amazing facts

- The phylum Arthropoda gets its name from two Greek words, *arthros* meaning 'joint' and *podos* meaning 'foot'.
- Some arthropods, such as crustaceans and mygalomorph spiders (tarantulas and funnel-web spiders), moult throughout their lives, but in insects it is usually just the **larvae** that moult.
- During moulting, an arthropod is in greater danger of being attacked by a **predator**, as its body is soft and unprotected.

Insects

Insects first appeared about 300–550 million years ago and are thought to have **evolved** from myriapod-like ancestors. Many **species** of insects live on land, but large numbers are found in freshwater habitats such as lakes, rivers and ponds. Most insects are small and their tough **exoskeleton** prevents them from losing water, which means they can survive in dry conditions. Insects with wings can travel long distances in search of food, **mates** and suitable places to live, which means they are found in a wide range of habitats.

An insect's body is made up of three parts: the head, the **thorax** and the **abdomen**. The head bears the mouthparts, a pair of **compound eyes** and one pair of **antennae**. The main **characteristics** that separate the insects from other arthropods are that they have three pairs of jointed legs and usually one or two pairs of wings attached to the thorax. The abdomen is segmented and does not have any **appendages**.

Sense organs

Insects have well-developed sense organs. The antennae are sensitive to touch and to chemicals in the environment. Insects use their antennae to give them information about food sources, finding mates and recognizing members of their own species. The large compound eyes are made up of many thousands of tiny structures, called ommatidia, each with its own lens. Each lens points in a slightly different direction and each forms an image. The images formed are not sharply defined, but the insect can detect movements and shapes. There are other sense organs in the **cuticle** and on the limbs, which respond to touch and chemicals.

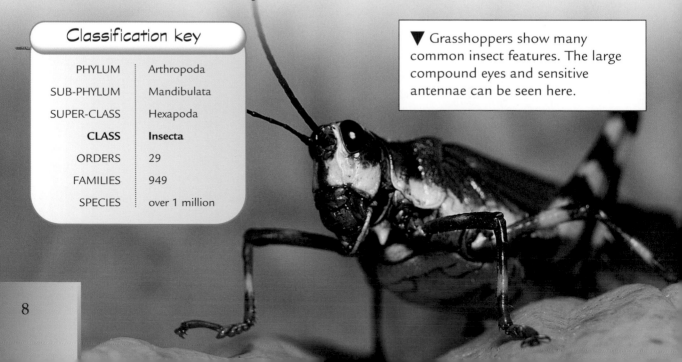

Classification key

PHYLUM	Arthropoda
SUB-PHYLUM	Mandibulata
SUPER-CLASS	Hexapoda
CLASS	**Insecta**
ORDERS	29
FAMILIES	949
SPECIES	over 1 million

▼ Grasshoppers show many common insect features. The large compound eyes and sensitive antennae can be seen here.

Non-insect hexapods

Having three pairs of legs places insects in the super-class Hexapoda, together with collembolans, proturans and diplurans. These three groups are known as non-insect hexapods and are found all over the world. The collembolans, such as *Sminthus viridis,* and the proturans, such as *Eosentomon delicatum*, are about 2 millimetres long and live in soil and leaf litter. The diplurans, such as the common North American species *Catajapyx diversiunguis*, are larger. None of these groups has wings and many lack eyes and antennae. Their mouthparts are in a pouch underneath the head.

Classification key

PHYLUM	Arthropoda
SUB-PHYLUM	Mandibulata
SUPER-CLASS	Hexapoda
CLASS	**Collembola**
FAMILIES	18
SPECIES	6500
CLASS	**Protura**
FAMILIES	4
SPECIES	400
CLASS	**Diplura**
FAMILIES	9
SPECIES	800

Amazing facts

- Insects were the first creatures to live on land and appeared about 200 million years before the dinosaurs.
- The world's longest insect is the giant stick insect of Indonesia, which grows to a length of about 30 centimetres.

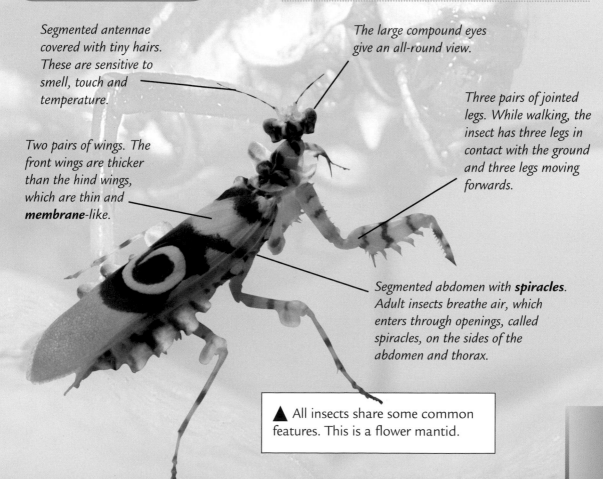

Segmented antennae covered with tiny hairs. These are sensitive to smell, touch and temperature.

The large compound eyes give an all-round view.

Two pairs of wings. The front wings are thicker than the hind wings, which are thin and **membrane**-like.

Three pairs of jointed legs. While walking, the insect has three legs in contact with the ground and three legs moving forwards.

Segmented abdomen with **spiracles**. Adult insects breathe air, which enters through openings, called spiracles, on the sides of the abdomen and thorax.

▲ All insects share some common features. This is a flower mantid.

Insect life cycles

Insects lay eggs, which hatch into **larvae**. The larvae feed, grow rapidly and undergo several **moults** before they become adults and are able to **breed**. The change from larva to adult is called **metamorphosis**.

▶ Caterpillars, such as this vapourer moth caterpillar, are larvae that begin eating as soon as they hatch. They grow rapidly and moult several times.

Metamorphosis

In some insects, such as locusts, the eggs hatch into larvae called **nymphs**. Locust nymphs look very similar to the adults, but do not have wings. Instead, there are little pads or buds where the wings will develop later. As the larvae grow, they moult. After the final moult, the mature insect emerges, complete with wings. This type of metamorphosis, with only three life-cycle stages, is called incomplete metamorphosis.

Other insects, such as butterflies and beetles, have four distinct life-cycle stages – egg, larva, **pupa** and adult. This type of metamorphosis is called complete metamorphosis. The eggs hatch into larvae, which are called grubs, maggots or caterpillars, depending on the **species**. The larvae feed and moult several times, growing rapidly until they reach their full size. They then enter the pupal stage, where all the larval body parts break down and the adult ones are formed. During this stage, the insect is inactive and does not feed. In many insects, the pupal stage takes place inside a protective case, called a **cocoon** or **chrysalis**. When the adult emerges from the pupa, it is fully mature and able to breed.

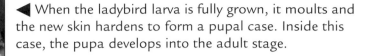

◄ When the ladybird larva is fully grown, it moults and the new skin hardens to form a pupal case. Inside this case, the pupa develops into the adult stage.

Larvae

Larvae represent the feeding and growing stages in the life cycle. Their way of life, food, method of **locomotion** and habitat are usually very different from the adults of the same species. In some species, such as caddis flies, the larvae are **aquatic**, whereas the adults live on land and are able to fly. The length of time taken to complete the life cycle varies from one species to another and can also depend on the time of year. Aquatic larvae, such as mayfly larvae, may take a year or more to develop into adults. The adults survive for only a few hours, long enough to **mate** and lay eggs.

Amazing facts

- Female butterflies 'stamp' on the leaves of a plant, to test if they are ripe enough to lay their eggs on.
- Periodical cicadas, found in the USA, may take from thirteen to seventeen years to become adults and able to breed.
- In dragonflies, the larval stage may last several years. The nymphs are aquatic and feed on tadpoles and young fish.

▲ Just before an adult dragonfly emerges, the chrysalis becomes darker. The adult's wings are crumpled at first. It pumps blood into the veins of the wings to straighten them out.

Insect flight

Insects are the only **invertebrates** that are able to fly. Winged insects can travel long distances in search of food, **mates** and new habitats. They are able to escape from their enemies and move to more favourable conditions quickly. These factors have contributed to their success as a group.

Wings

Insects' wings are flattened extensions of the **cuticle**, which forms the **exoskeleton**. They are strengthened and supported by a network of veins. Most winged insects have two pairs of wings attached to the **thorax**. The base of each wing is situated between the plates, or sclerites, that form the top and sides of the exoskeleton. In flight, the wing moves like a see-saw. Its position means that a small amount of muscle movement causes a large movement of the wing.

In some insects, such as dragonflies and butterflies, the two pairs of wings are similar. In other groups, such as beetles and cockroaches, the front wings are hard or leathery, and protect the thinner, **membrane**-like hind wings. True flies (Diptera) have front wings that are thin and membrane-like, but their hind wings have **adapted** to form a pair of small, club-shaped structures, called **halteres**. These act as balancing organs, helping the fly to keep on its course and to make rapid changes in direction.

▲ The hardened front wings of beetles, such as the ladybird, are called elytra. They protect the delicate hind wings when the beetle is not flying.

Amazing facts

- The buzzing of a fly is the sound of its wings beating. The wings of midges beat about 1000 times a second.
- Butterflies may bask in the sun to warm up their wing muscles before flying. The wings absorb energy like solar panels.

Flight muscles

Dragonflies have flight muscles attached to the base of their wings and also to the thorax. When the muscles attached to the wings contract, the wings are pushed downwards. This is called a downstroke. An upstroke occurs when the muscles attached to the thorax contract. Beetles and butterflies do not have flight muscles directly attached to the wings. Instead, wing movements are brought about by muscle contraction changing the shape of the thorax.

Many insects need to beat their wings very rapidly in order to stay in the air. This type of flight uses up a great deal of energy. Butterflies and moths fly in a different way. They flap their wings slowly up and down, like birds, and can use **air currents** to keep them up in the air.

▶ True flies, such as this dronefly, have a single pair of thin, membrane-like front wings.

▲ Adult locusts gather together in large groups, called swarms, and fly to new feeding grounds.

Butterflies and moths

Butterflies and moths are found worldwide, with the exception of Antarctica. They all have two pairs of wings covered in tiny scales and undergo complete **metamorphosis** (see pages 10–11) during their life cycle. In general, butterflies are brightly coloured, have clubbed **antennae** and are active during the day. Their bodies are thin and relatively hairless, and they settle with their wings folded so that the undersides are exposed. Moths usually have fatter, hairy bodies and their antennae are often feathery, but never clubbed. They fly at dusk or during the night. When they settle, their wings are spread flat, with the upper surface showing. Many moths are dull coloured, but several have brightly coloured wings and spectacular markings.

Feeding

Adult butterflies and moths feed on **nectar** and other liquids through a long sucking tube, called the **proboscis**, which is coiled under the head when not in use. Butterfly **larvae**, called caterpillars, have biting mouthparts, called **mandibles**, so that they can chew plant material. Adults do not have mandibles. Caterpillars feed all the time and their numerous legs give them a firm hold on their food. They have three pairs of true legs on the **thorax** and five pairs of fleshy pro-legs (legs without joints) on the **abdomen**.

Classification key	
PHYLUM	Arthropoda
SUB-PHYLUM	Mandibulata
SUPER-CLASS	Hexapoda
CLASS	Insecta
ORDER	**Lepidoptera**
FAMILIES	127
SPECIES	about 165,000

▼ The amazing colours of the Asian comet moth's wings are due to the covering of scales. Each scale is a tiny flattened hair, which is either coloured or reflects the light in a certain way, giving an overall brilliant effect.

This moth caterpillar is brightly coloured and is covered in tiny bristles to put off **predators**.

Mating

Adult butterflies and moths only live long enough to **mate** and for the females to lay their eggs. Males and females produce chemical substances, or scents, called pheromones, to attract the opposite sex. Females have scent glands on the abdomen and the males produce scents from special scales on the wings. A female mates once and then produces a special scent, which stops other males from mating with her. Males mate several times.

Skippers

Skippers are different from most butterflies and share some **characteristics** with moths. They have hooked, not clubbed, antennae and plump, hairy bodies. They get their name from their darting flight, beating their wings rapidly, and their ability to change direction suddenly. Like many moths, their **pupae** are encased in a **cocoon**.

Amazing facts

- Queen Alexandra's birdwing butterfly, found only in New Guinea, is the world's largest butterfly. Females may have a wingspan of up to 28 centimetres.

- The smallest butterfly in the world is the pygmy blue with a wingspan of between 11 and 18 millimetres.

- The caterpillars of the orchard swallowtail butterfly are **camouflaged** to look like bird droppings. This **adaptation** helps them to escape their enemies.

▶ A butterfly's proboscis unfurls like a drinking straw to suck up the nectar. It is extended by an increase in the butterfly's blood pressure.

The monarch butterfly

The monarch butterfly is most common in North, Central and South America. Adult American monarchs have bright orange wings with black veins and outer margins and have a wingspan of about 10 centimetres. Their bodies are black with white spots. Both **larvae** and adults feed on a plant called milkweed, which contains chemicals that are poisonous to their **predators**. The adults feed on the **nectar** in the flowers and the larvae eat the leaves.

Life cycle

The female butterfly lays her eggs on the underside of milkweed leaves. They take about three to fifteen days to hatch. The caterpillar eats its way out of the egg and then begins to feed on the milkweed leaves. It continues to feed for the next fifteen days, during which time it will **moult** four times.

When it has reached about 5 centimetres long, the caterpillar stops feeding, finds a branch and attaches itself by means of a silk pad. It moults one last time and its skin then hardens to form the **pupa**, or **chrysalis**. Inside the pupa, the larval body parts break down and the adult ones are formed. This stage takes about ten to twelve days. The chrysalis splits down the back and the adult butterfly emerges.

Adult monarch butterflies are ready to **mate** about three to eight days after emerging from the chrysalis. They may mate several times during their lives. The females begin to lay their eggs immediately after mating.

▼ Milkweed plants contain a poisonous substance, which is absorbed by the bodies of monarch caterpillars. The poison protects them from being eaten by **vertebrate** predators such as birds and mice.

Classification key

PHYLUM	Arthropoda
SUB-PHYLUM	Mandibulata
SUPER-CLASS	Hexapoda
CLASS	Insecta
ORDER	Lepidoptera
FAMILIES	Danaidae
GENUS	*Danaus*
SPECIES	***Danaus plexippus***

Amazing facts

- Large **colonies** of migrating butterflies are found in Mexico. Between 15,000 and 20,000 monarch butterflies may roost on one tree branch.

- In order to follow the migration, scientists have glued tiny paper tags on to the wings of the butterflies. One butterfly tagged in Minnesota, USA, flew to Mexico, a distance of 3122 kilometres (1844 miles).

▶ Monarch butterflies feed on nectar. They visit a range of different flowers including milkweed, clover and thistles.

Migration

In the northern states of the USA and in southern Canada the butterflies **breed** during the summer. In autumn, as the weather gets colder, most of the adult butterflies **migrate** to the southern USA and Mexico, where they spend the winter, often gathering in large numbers. In the spring, they start to return north. As these adults migrate north, they mate and produce offspring. Several generations of butterflies will be born during the migration north. So a different generation of butterflies returns to the northern states of the USA and southern Canada. The lifespan of the adult butterflies that emerge in the autumn is about eight months, but those that are produced during the spring and summer months, on the return migration, only live for about four to six weeks.

▶ Hibernating butterflies form dense clusters on trees. Each hangs with its wings down over the one below it. This provides protection from rain and helps to keep the group warm.

Ants, bees and wasps

The insects in the order Hymenoptera have two pairs of delicate, **membranous** wings, with the front pair larger than the hind pair. The wings are coupled together with a row of hooks on the front edge of the hind wings.

▶ Bees collect nectar and pollen from flowers. As the bees visit the flowers, they transfer pollen from one plant to another and bring about pollination.

Characteristic features

Ants, bees and wasps, together with the ichneumon flies, belong to the sub-order Apocrita. They have a narrow 'waist' between the **thorax** and the **abdomen**. The mouthparts are **adapted** for biting, but they can also take up liquids, such as **nectar** from flowers. The **larvae** are legless with small heads. Female bees, wasps and some ants have stings at the tips of the abdomen.

Sawflies belong to the sub-order Symphyta. They do not have a narrow 'waist' between the thorax and the abdomen. They do not sting, and their larvae are similar to caterpillars, with definite heads, legs and pro-legs. They show no social behaviour and none are **parasites**.

▲ Two pairs of delicate wings and a definite 'waist' between the thorax and the abdomen are **characteristic** of bees (seen above storing collected nectar into the honey cells of a comb) and wasps.

Social insects

Many ants, bees and wasps live in large groups, or **colonies**, where all the individuals belong to the same family and are often the offspring of a single female. They are known as social insects. There are usually several different types of individuals, or **castes**, in one colony, all performing different jobs. In a honey bee colony, there is one egg-laying female, called the queen, several thousand **sterile** females called worker bees and a few hundred male bees, or drones. Males develop from **unfertilized** eggs. Their function is to **mate** with the queen. These drones are fed by the workers from stores of nectar and pollen and live for only a few weeks. Fertilized eggs hatch into larvae, which may develop into workers or queens depending on the food they are given. Larvae that are to become queens are fed on royal jelly, a rich substance that comes from the workers, until they **pupate**. Larvae that will develop into workers are given dilute nectar and pollen after three days. The workers collect nectar and pollen, look after the larvae, clean the hive and feed the queen.

Amazing facts

- Wasps do not make honey, but feed on nectar, the juices of fruits or smaller creatures.
- The sting of a honey bee is barbed. It cannot be withdrawn from human skin without leaving behind the barb and **venom** sac. This damages the abdomen of the bee and she dies.

Classification key

PHYLUM	Arthropoda
SUB-PHYLUM	Mandibulata
SUPER-CLASS	Hexapoda
CLASS	Insecta
ORDER	Hymenoptera
SUB-ORDER	**Symphyta (sawflies) Apocrita (ants, bees and wasps)**
FAMILIES	91
SPECIES	at least 198,000

▼ Leaf-cutter ants feed on fungus, which they grow in their underground nests. They grow the fungus on pieces of leaves, which they collect and take back to the nest.

Termites

Most **species** of termite live in the **tropics**, but a few are found in southern Europe and in the USA. Termites resemble true ants and are often confused with them. However, true ants have a 'waist' between their **thorax** and **abdomen**, while termites do not. True ants are related to bees and wasps, but termites are more closely related to cockroaches.

Castes

Termite **colonies** contain four types of **caste**. There is usually one fertile, egg-laying queen and a male 'king', who **fertilizes** the eggs. There are very large numbers of small, **sterile**, wingless males and females with whitish bodies called workers. They build the nest, find food, groom other members of the colony and look after the eggs. In addition, there are soldiers, also sterile and wingless, but with enlarged heads bearing huge jaws or long snouts. They guard the colony and protect the workers when they are out collecting food.

Classification key

PHYLUM	Arthropoda
SUB-PHYLUM	Mandibulata
SUPER-CLASS	Hexapoda
CLASS	Insecta
ORDER	Isoptera
FAMILY	**Termitidae**
SPECIES	1950

▶ Termite mounds are constructed of soil cemented with saliva and baked in the sun. Inside there are many chambers connected by passages and ducts to allow the air to circulate.

Forming new colonies

At certain times, winged male and female termites develop in the colonies. These have harder, darker bodies and **compound eyes**. When they are mature, they fly off in swarms and pair up to start new colonies. After their flight, they shed their wings and **mate**. The female lays eggs and becomes queen of the new colony. Her abdomen becomes swollen with thousands of eggs and in some species she grows many times larger than a normal female. The eggs hatch into **nymphs**, which look like the adults. They go through an incomplete **metamorphosis** (see page 10), becoming more like the adults after each **moult**.

▲ The queen becomes very large, up to 10 centimetres long in some species.

The king and queen produce special chemical substances to stop the workers producing their own offspring, which would compete for food and living space with those of the king and queen. The workers lick these substances off the bodies of the king and queen and pass them on to other members of the colony during grooming. When the queen dies these substances run out, causing some nymphs to develop reproductive organs and enabling them to produce offspring.

▲ The soldier termites guard and protect the worker termites while they gather food for the colony.

Amazing facts

- In west Africa, fat juicy termite queens are eaten by humans. In some countries, insects are considered tasty and nourishing additions to the diet.
- In species where she becomes very large, (such as *Macrotermes*) a queen termite may lay 30,000 eggs in a day.
- A colony can contain several hundred to several million termites.

Bugs

Bugs form a very large order of insects called Hemiptera, found all over the world. They vary in size from tiny whiteflies, which are about 3 millimetres long, to large cicadas, which have a wingspan of up to 15 centimetres. All bugs have two pairs of wings and slender, needle-like mouthparts for piercing and sucking their food. Their eggs hatch into **nymphs**, which feed on the same kind of food as the adults. Adults and nymphs are often found together. The nymphs grow into adults by incomplete **metamorphosis** (see page 10).

Bugs or beetles?

Many bugs, such as shield bugs or stink bugs, look like beetles, but their mouthparts and front wings are different. All beetles have biting mouthparts. The front wings of a beetle meet in the middle. The whole of the front wing is hard and forms a protective covering for the hind wings. The ends of the front wings of a bug overlap, and the tips of these wings are **membranous**.

▼ Male cicadas make shrill noises, or 'sing', by rapidly vibrating two small membranes on either side of the **abdomen** to attract females or warn off enemies.

Amazing facts

- All species of the genus of pond skaters *Halobates* are marine and live on the surface of tropical and sub-tropical seas. They lay their eggs on floating seaweed.
- The red food dye cochineal is extracted from a species of scale insect, the cochineal bug. It was first used by the Aztecs in Mexico hundreds of years ago.
- The male cicadas in some species produce calls that can be heard 1.5 kilometres (0.9 miles) away.

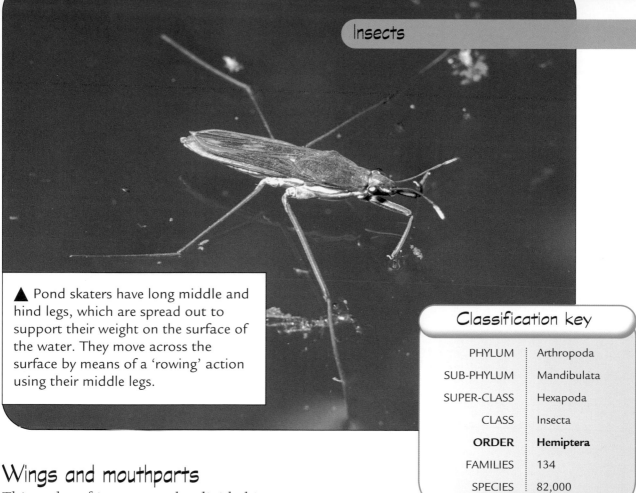

▲ Pond skaters have long middle and hind legs, which are spread out to support their weight on the surface of the water. They move across the surface by means of a 'rowing' action using their middle legs.

Classification key

PHYLUM	Arthropoda
SUB-PHYLUM	Mandibulata
SUPER-CLASS	Hexapoda
CLASS	Insecta
ORDER	**Hemiptera**
FAMILIES	134
SPECIES	82,000

Wings and mouthparts

This order of insects can be divided into two groups, according to differences in wing structure and in the position of the beak like mouthparts called the **rostrum**. In the group (Heteroptera) that contains the shield bugs, the front wings are divided into two parts. The part that is attached to the body is tough and leathery, and the tip is delicate and membranous. The rostrum is found at the front of the head. This group includes capsid bugs, bedbugs and all the **aquatic species**, such as pond skaters.

Cicadas, leaf hoppers and aphids belong to the group Homoptera. In this group the rostrum comes from the back part of the head and the front wings are not divided. They are either completely stiffened or completely membranous. Cicadas and leaf hoppers have short, bristle-like **antennae**, but aphids, whiteflies and male scale insects have long, thread-like antennae. Female scale insects do not have legs, wings or antennae. They have bodies covered by a hard scale, giving the group its name. The males have wings but lack scales and look like tiny midges.

▲ Shield bugs get their name from their flattened shape, which looks like a shield.

Beetles

There are more known **species** of beetle in the world than any other insect. They are found in a wide range of habitats on land and in water. This group includes aphid-eating ladybirds, dung beetles and the **aquatic** whirligig beetles. Their success is due to the tough **cuticle** that covers their bodies. They all have hard front wings, called elytra, which protect the delicate **membranous** hind wings. They can live under stones, in litter and in water. They are not easily damaged and they can survive in dry places because the tough cuticle stops their bodies from losing water. They all have biting jaws. The jaws are used for feeding, but in some species they have been **adapted** for fighting. There is also some variation in the structure of the legs, which may be used for walking, swimming or digging.

▲ The bright colours of the forewings (elytra) are a signal to **predators** that this beetle has a nasty taste.

Classification key

PHYLUM	Arthropoda
SUB-PHYLUM	Mandibulata
SUPER-CLASS	Hexapoda
CLASS	Insecta
ORDER	**Coleoptera**
FAMILIES	166
SPECIES	370,000

▲ Weevils are sometimes called snout beetles. The head has a beak-shaped structure, called a **rostrum**, with a pair of jaws (**mandibles**) at the tip.

Beetle life cycle

The beetle life cycle involves a complete **metamorphosis**. Beetles may lay their eggs near a food source for the **larvae**, but some just scatter the eggs. The larvae, usually called grubs, do not look like their parents. They look like worms, but have well-developed heads with biting jaws similar to the adults. Adults and larvae are often found on the same food source. The larvae feed and grow, **moulting** several times, before entering the **pupal** stage. When the adult beetle emerges from the pupa, it is ready to **breed**.

The length of the beetle life cycle varies from one species to another. In some beetles, such as ladybirds, it takes from five to eight weeks to complete the cycle from egg to adult. Stag beetles' eggs hatch after two weeks, but the larval stage can last up to five years.

Amazing facts

- A click beetle can jump 30 centimetres into the air.

- In severe winter conditions, it is too cold for most adult insects to survive. The eggs of beetles, such as the tiger beetle, are buried in the soil. There the eggs are insulated from the freezing temperatures, until the larvae are ready to hatch out the following spring.

- Female glow-worms (*Lampyris noctiluca*) are wingless. On the underside of the last three segments of the **abdomen**, they have light-producing organs to attract males flying near by at night.

▼ Male stag beetles are larger than the females. They use their huge antler-like mandibles to fight other males during the breeding season.

Dragonflies and damselflies

Dragonflies and damselflies are large, winged insects found in wetlands all over the world. They have two pairs of large, transparent wings, a pair of **compound eyes**, a pair of short **antennae** and a long, often brightly-coloured, **abdomen**. The wings can move independently, allowing the insect to speed up, brake, hover and steer with great accuracy. The eyes are very large and prominent, detecting movements easily, so these insects can track and catch their **prey** whilst they are flying.

Incomplete metamorphosis

Female dragonflies lay their eggs in freshwater ponds, lakes and slow-flowing streams. Some **species** lay their eggs on or in water plants, while others just scatter them. The eggs hatch into wingless **nymphs**, which remain in the water throughout their development. This may last from one to five years. They breathe using **gills**.

▶ The damselfly rests with its wings folded. It tends to stay near water.

Classification key

PHYLUM	Arthropoda
SUB-PHYLUM	Mandibulata
SUPER-CLASS	Hexapoda
CLASS	Insecta
ORDER	**Odonata**
FAMILIES	30
SPECIES	about 5500

Amazing facts

- The compound eye of a dragonfly has about 30,000 lenses.
- Dragonflies can fly at speeds of 95–100 kilometres (59–62 miles) per hour.

The nymphs are meat eaters, or **carnivores**, like the adults. They hunt their prey under water, feeding on other **larvae**, tadpoles and even small fish. The lower lip is elongated and hinged in the middle, with two movable claws at the end. The whole structure is called a 'mask' and is tucked under the head when not in use. When suitable prey is seen, the mask is pushed forwards and the food captured by the claws.

▲ Dragonflies have two pairs of powerful wings. In contrast to the damselfly, the wings are spread out when at rest.

When fully grown, the nymph crawls up the stem of a water plant and out of the water. It **moults** for the last time and emerges as an adult with wings. The adults live for a few weeks. They are powerful fliers, catching their prey of mosquitoes and other small insects as they fly. Male dragonflies search out the females and **mating** occurs on land. The male grasps hold of the female and the pair may fly around together after mating. The female either lays her eggs in the tissues of water plants or flies across the surface of water dipping the tip of her abdomen into the water at intervals and scattering her eggs.

Dragonflies or damselflies?

Adult dragonflies and damselflies look quite similar. The main differences between the adults are in the structure of the wings and the abdomen. Damselflies have wings that are alike, but dragonflies have hind wings that are broader than the front wings. Dragonflies are generally bigger, with a fatter abdomen. They fly faster and may travel several kilometres from water. Damselflies are more slender and delicate, with slower and less powerful flight. Damselfly nymphs have external gills, situated at the end of the abdomen. Dragonfly nymphs have gills inside the end of the abdomen.

▲ This close-up of the head of a dragonfly shows the large compound eyes that give good all-round vision and help the insect to track its prey.

Flies

Dipterans, or true flies, form one of the largest orders of insects. They are found all over the world, ranging in size from midges just a few millimetres long to horseflies with bodies up to 2.5 centimetres in length. True flies are liquid feeders and have piercing or sucking mouthparts.

True flies are the only insects to have just one pair of wings. The hind wings are reduced to a pair of **halteres** (see page 12). They help to keep the flight of the fly straight and level. A few **species**, such as the **parasitic** Sheep Ked, do not have wings. The order is divided into those species, such as crane flies, mosquitoes and gnats, that have long **antennae** with several segments, and those that have shorter antennae with only two or three segments, such as the housefly. All the dipterans have a life cycle that involves complete **metamorphosis**.

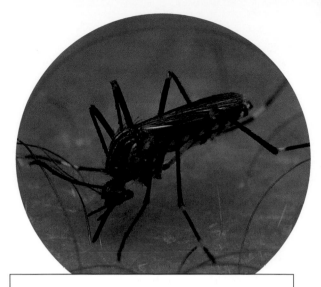

▲ Female mosquitoes have syringe-like mouthparts **adapted** for piercing the skin of mammals and birds. Males have sucking mouthparts and feed on nectar.

Amazing facts

- Houseflies have taste sensors on their feet to detect suitable sources of food.
- Some of the largest flies in the family Mydeidae are up to 60 millimetres long.
- A housefly can reach a speed of about 7 kilometres (4 miles) per hour when flying.

Classification key

PHYLUM	Arthropoda
SUB-PHYLUM	Mandibulata
SUPER-CLASS	Hexapoda
CLASS	Insecta
ORDER	**Diptera**
FAMILIES	130
SPECIES	122,000

◄ Houseflies have chunky bodies, short antennae with bristles and a pair of large **compound eyes**. Their wings are transparent and have few veins.

Feeding habits

Depending on the species, food sources include decaying plant and animal remains, **nectar** and plant sap, or blood from mammals and birds. Those that feed on blood have sharp, piercing mouthparts to get through the skin of their victims. Female mosquitoes have mouthparts that fit together to form a tube, with which the flesh is pierced and blood can be sucked up. Other blood-sucking flies, such as horseflies and stable flies, have similar sharp structures. Houseflies suck up liquid food through a fleshy **proboscis**, which has many tiny channels in it. If they feed on solid food, they may produce saliva containing digestive juices over it first, to break down the food into liquid and then suck it up.

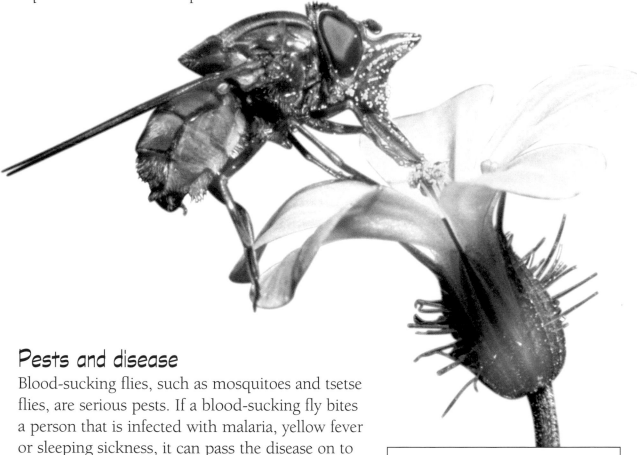

Pests and disease

Blood-sucking flies, such as mosquitoes and tsetse flies, are serious pests. If a blood-sucking fly bites a person that is infected with malaria, yellow fever or sleeping sickness, it can pass the disease on to the blood of the next person that it bites.

Houseflies can contaminate human food. They may feed on manure or rubbish and then come into contact with human food afterwards. Houseflies often **regurgitate** some of their previous meal when feeding and this can spread harmful bacteria and diseases such as typhoid and cholera.

▲ Hoverflies feed on pollen and nectar. They have brightly coloured bodies and many species look like bees or wasps, but they do not sting.

Crustacea

Most **crustaceans** are **aquatic**, ranging in size from tiny **organisms** such as water fleas to large crabs and lobsters. In the larger crustaceans, the **exoskeleton** is usually hard and thickened with calcium carbonate, except at the joints. Within the group there is a great deal of variation in body shape. Usually the body is divided into head, **thorax** and **abdomen**, but in many **species** the head is fused with the thorax to form a **cephalothorax**. A shield-like outgrowth from the head, called the **carapace**, extends back over the body and protects the **gills**.

In a typical crustacean, the head has two pairs of **antennae**, one pair of **compound eyes** on stalks, and paired mouthparts. The segments of the cephalothorax and the abdomen each bear a pair of limbs. These may be **adapted** for swimming, crawling or feeding. There is sometimes a tail portion, called the **telson**, which is used in swimming. Not all these features are seen in every class. For example, body segments are not clearly seen in water fleas, and barnacles have a very reduced head and abdomen.

Classification key	
PHYLUM	Arthropoda
SUB-PHYLUM	Mandibulata
SUPER-CLASS	**Crustacea**
CLASSES	6 – Branchiopoda (water fleas and brine shrimps); Ostracoda (oyster shrimps); Maxillopoda (copepods and barnacles); Malacostraca (crabs, lobsters and prawns); Remipedia (eyeless, primitive forms); Cephalocarida (tiny, shrimp-like forms)
ORDERS	37
FAMILIES	540
SPECIES	more than 40,000

▼ The stalked eyes of this Australian mud crab give an all-round view of its surroundings. The tough exoskeleton and well-developed claws are also typical of this group of crustaceans.

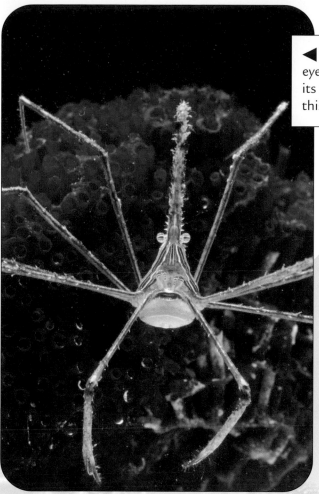

With its long, slender legs and prominent eyes, it is easy to see how the spider crab got its name. Despite its fearsome appearance, this crab feeds on sponges and seaweeds.

Larval forms

Most crustacean eggs hatch into minute **larvae**, which are very different from the adults. The simplest types of larvae are not segmented, but they have three pairs of **appendages**, which they use for movement as well as feeding. In some species, like water fleas, these larvae feed, grow and **moult**, each time looking more like the adults. In other species, such as barnacles and crabs, the larvae are free-swimming and there may be two or more different larval stages. In groups where the adults are fixed in one place, such as barnacles, or slow-moving, such as crabs, free-swimming larvae are important in spreading to new areas and moving to suitable habitats.

Amazing facts

- The pill woodlouse, *Armadillidium vulgare*, can roll itself into a ball to escape **predators**. It is also thought that this reduces water loss and prevents the animal from drying up.
- Water fleas get their name because the movements of their antennae make them appear to be hopping like a flea.
- In the USA, woodlice are used by museum workers to clean the flesh from delicate **vertebrate skeletons**.

▶ Woodlice are found in clusters under stones and in damp places. They have seven pairs of walking legs on the thorax and appendages on the abdomen that are used for breathing.

Crabs and lobsters

Crabs and lobsters belong to a large group of **crustaceans** called the Malacostraca. They are found all over the world from the open seas and seashores to freshwater and land habitats. Usually, they have tough **exoskeletons**, eyes on stalks and prominent **antennae**. There are eight segments in the **thorax** and six segments in the

abdomen. The first pair of walking legs on the thorax usually has large claws, or pincers, at the end for holding and tearing food. At the end of the abdomen, there may be a tail fan, or **telson**, which is used in swimming. The head and thorax, forming the **cephalothorax**, are covered by the **carapace**. Underneath the carapace, there are feathery **gills**. On the abdomen, there are often **appendages** that are used for swimming, **mating** or holding the eggs until they hatch.

◀ The large, well-developed pincers of this common lobster are used for holding **prey** and tearing food.

Crawlers

Crabs and lobsters are crawlers, rather than swimmers. They all have a heavy exoskeleton, which prevents them moving rapidly in water but protects them from **predators**. In this group, there are lobsters and crayfish, squat lobsters and true crabs. The lobsters and crayfish have long antennae, a large abdomen and a broad telson. If alarmed, a lobster can bend its abdomen and use its telson to move backwards suddenly. The squat lobsters have a smaller abdomen and no telson, but they can still swim backwards to get away from their enemies. The true crabs have a much smaller abdomen, which is bent forward underneath, so that only the flattened carapace is seen. The antennae are short and the pincers are always well developed.

Classification key	
PHYLUM	Arthropoda
SUB-PHYLUM	Mandibulata
SUPER-CLASS	Crustacea
CLASS	**Malacostraca**
ORDER	Decapoda
SPECIES	20,000

Spider crabs

Spider crabs are true crabs. Their carapace is extended to form a spiny projection, called the **rostrum**. They have extremely long legs in relation to the size of their body. They use their pincers, which are quite small, to cover themselves with seaweed so that they can hide from predators. They range in size from the yellowline arrow crab (up to 6 centimetres long) to the enormous Japanese island crab, whose legs may reach 1.5 metres long.

▼ Hermit crabs live in the empty shells of sea snails. As the crabs grow, they get too big for the shell and must move to a new home.

Amazing facts

- About 100 million red crabs live on Christmas Island in the Indian Ocean. Every year they **migrate** from their homes inland to the coast, where they mate and produce their eggs.
- The robber crab, *Birgus latro*, lives on islands in the Pacific and climbs palm trees to feed on the coconuts.

▼ This tiny spider crab is found in the Atlantic Ocean. The males mate with the females and then stay to drive other males away.

Common shore crab

The common shore crab is a typical example of a true crab. It is found in mud flats and sandy regions of the shore, as well as in rock pools in Europe and North America. Like all true crabs, it has a thick **carapace** covering the **cephalothorax**. The **abdomen** is a flap, which is tucked underneath the body. The common shore crab has a pair of pincers with **serrated** edges, which it uses to grab hold of small animals and other food. It has four pairs of walking legs.

The fourth pair is **adapted** for swimming, and is more flattened and paddle-like than the other three pairs. On its head the crab has short **antennae**, **compound eyes** on stalks and a pair of strong jaws (**mandibles**), which are used to hold food. Other mouthparts then shred the food and push it into the mouth.

Amazing facts

- Crab larvae form part of the large number of tiny **organisms** found in the surface layers of the sea. These organisms form the **zooplankton** (animal **plankton**), which is the food of fish such as herrings.
- All the larval stages of crabs have prominent eyes on stalks.
- Male crabs are quite aggressive and will fight each other for the chance to mate with a female.

▼ This female Christmas Island red crab has a large, dark-coloured mass of fertilized eggs attached to her abdomen.

34

◀ Although the larvae of crabs are adapted for swimming, an adult crab moves slowly in water.

Breeding and life cycle

Mating occurs between male and female crabs just after the female has **moulted**. The **fertilized** eggs are protected by being carried around on the abdomen of the female. The eggs are held by special branched **appendages** on the underside of the abdomen. These appendages have tiny spines, called setae, on them for the attachment of the eggs. The mass of eggs is yellow-orange in colour. The eggs hatch out into **larvae**, which are called zoea. These are tiny and do not look like crabs at all. They have a slender, curved abdomen and a carapace with two long spines on it, one pointing forwards and one backwards. Each larva swims around, feeds, grows, and moults several times. As it grows, it develops limbs on the **thorax** and on the abdomen and changes into the next larval stage, called the megalopa. This stage looks much more like a crab. It comes to the surface and swims around, before moulting to become a fully-formed crab. It is at this last moult that the flap of the abdomen folds under the body and is no longer used for swimming.

▲ These crab larvae swim freely, feed and grow, moulting several times before they develop into the adult form.

Prawns and shrimps

True prawns and shrimps belong to the same order as crabs and lobsters (Decapoda), and share many of their **characteristics**. With their long **abdomen**, they look more like lobsters than crabs. Prawns and shrimps are swimmers, rather than crawlers. They have lighter **exoskeletons** and their bodies are flattened from side to side, allowing them to move easily through water. Prawns and shrimps are found all over the world in both freshwater and marine habitats.

The decapod prawns and shrimps are transparent or greenish-brown in colour. They have a well-developed, muscular abdomen with a broad **telson**, which is used in swimming. There are eight pairs of **appendages** on the **thorax**. The first three pairs are mouthparts, used in feeding. The other five pairs of appendages are used for walking. On the abdomen, there are five pairs of short swimming legs, called pleopods.

Amazing facts

- Baleen (whalebone) whales **migrate** to Antarctic waters to feed on shoals of krill. One whale can eat as much as 2 tonnes of krill at one feeding session.
- In shoals of krill, there may be up to 20 kilograms of organisms per cubic metre.
- Krill have light-producing organs, which give off a greenish light, on their thorax.

Classification key

PHYLUM	Arthropoda
SUB-PHYLUM	Mandibulata
SUPER-CLASS	Crustacea
CLASS	Malacostraca
ORDERS	Amphipoda (freshwater shrimps)
	Decapoda (true prawns and shrimps)
	Stomatopoda (mantis shrimps)
	Euphausiacea (krill)

▲ Prawns have a well-developed rostrum, distinguishing them from edible shrimps. Both have a pair of long, backward-facing **antennae**.

Shrimp or prawn?

Prawns and shrimps have a **carapace** with a beak-like projection at the front, called the **rostrum**. In prawns, the rostrum is long and sometimes has a **serrated** (or toothed) edge. The rostrum of a shrimp is much smaller and looks like a spine. In many parts of the world, no distinction is made between the two, and the term 'shrimp' may be used for both.

▼ The mantis shrimp, found in **tropical** and sub-tropical seas, catches its **prey** using its second pair of legs. These are large and able to spear and crush small animals.

▼ The pistol shrimp has a large claw, which it uses to punch holes in the exoskeletons of **crustaceans**. The noise made by this claw as the pincers close gives the shrimp its name.

Freshwater shrimps, such as those in the genus *Gammarus*, belong to the order Amphipoda. They have bodies that are flattened from side to side. They can be found in freshwater streams, and around the stones on lower and middle seashores. Mantis shrimps belong to the order Stomatopoda, and get their name from their resemblance to the praying mantis.

Importance in food chains

Prawn and shrimp **larvae** form part of the **zooplankton** in **aquatic** habitats. The larvae, and the adults, feed on tiny **organisms** in the water and are, in their turn, eaten by larger organisms. The shrimp-like krill, belonging to the family Euphausiidae, are abundant in cooler oceans and are the main food of the baleen (whalebone) whales. There are about 85 different **species** of krill. They range in size from 8 to 70 millimetres long and are found on the surface as well as in deeper water. Krill feed on tiny plants, called diatoms, and are eaten by fish and birds as well as whales.

Copepods and barnacles

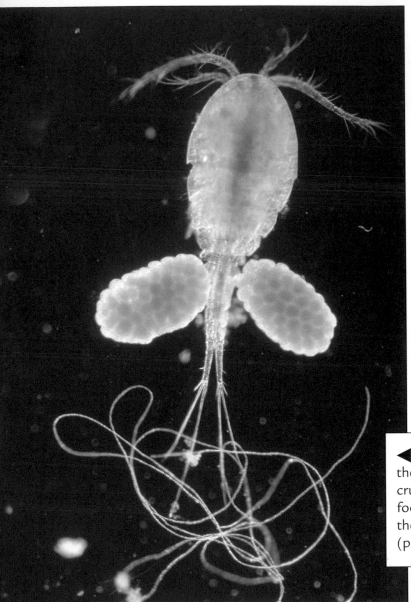

Copepods are tiny **aquatic crustaceans** found in large numbers in freshwater and marine habitats. They have a **cephalothorax**, but there is no **carapace** and there are no limbs on the **abdomen**. The adults and **larvae** form an important part of marine **plankton**, feeding on tiny plants and then themselves being the **prey** of larger aquatic **organisms** such as herrings. Some groups of copepods spend part of their life cycle as **parasites** attached to other animals, such as fish and whales. Others are free-living and are not parasitic as larvae or as adults.

◀ This freshwater copepod belongs to the genus *Cyclops*. It is a transparent crustacean with **mandibles** to break its food up into pieces. The females keep the fertilized eggs in a pair of egg sacs (pouches) on the abdomen.

Amazing facts

- *Cyclops* (a type of copepod with only one eye) get their name from the mythical giants that had a single eye in the middle of the forehead.
- Barnacles were originally thought to be related to molluscs until their larvae were identified and shown to be like those of other Crustacea.

Classification key

PHYLUM	Arthropoda
SUB-PHYLUM	Mandibulata
SUPER-CLASS	Crustacea
CLASS	Maxillopoda
ORDER	**Copepoda (copepods)**
FAMILIES	175

Barnacles

Barnacles are marine crustaceans. The adults live in groups attached to rocks, wood, ships' bottoms and the bodies of other animals, such as turtles and molluscs. They are found all over the world. The adult body is made up mostly of the **thorax**, surrounded by chalky plates of **exoskeleton**. The head and the abdomen are very small. They all have feathery thoracic limbs, called cirri, which they use to filter food from the water.

Acorn barnacles (*Balanus balanoides*) are often the most common animals on rocky shores. They are found in large numbers, encrusting rocks in the zone between high and low tide. The plates of the exoskeleton completely enclose the animal when it is not covered by water. When the tide comes in and covers the rocks, the top plates open and six pairs of cirri sweep through the water, filtering out food.

Barnacles are **hermaphrodites**, which means they have both male and female sex organs, but the eggs are **fertilized** by sperm cells from a neighbouring barnacle. The fertilized eggs are kept inside the animal and the larvae are only released when the conditions for survival are good. There are two types of larvae. The first is an unsegmented, simple larva, called a nauplius larva. This grows and **moults** several times, and eventually becomes a cypris larva. The cypris larva does not feed but finds a suitable place to settle. It anchors itself by producing a cement-like substance and then changes into the adult form.

▲ Goose barnacles (*Lepas* species) are bigger than acorn barnacles. They attach themselves to floating timbers and other supports by means of a flexible stalk.

Classification key

PHYLUM	Arthropoda
SUB-PHYLUM	Mandibulata
SUPER-CLASS	Crustacea
CLASS	Maxillopoda
ORDER	**Cirripedia (barnacles)**
FAMILIES	31
SPECIES	10,000

▶ Acorn barnacles attach themselves to rocks on the seashore. It has been estimated that there are over 50,000 per square metre on some shores.

Minor classes of crustacean

There are several minor classes of **crustacean**, many of which are of great importance in **aquatic food chains**. Some feed on dead **organic** material, others on tiny plants and algae, and a few feed on smaller arthropods.

Remipedia

This small group of crustaceans was not discovered until the 1980s. They are found in the Caribbean and Australia, in deep caves that connect with the sea. The body is divided into a head, which has **antennae** but no eyes, and a trunk section made up of 32 similar segments. Each segment has a pair of paddle-like **appendages** used for swimming.

Classification key	
PHYLUM	Arthropoda
SUB-PHYLUM	Mandibulata
SUPER-CLASS	Crustacea
CLASS	**Remipedia**
SPECIES	7

Branchiopoda

Branchiopods are usually found in fresh water, although some **species** can live in saltwater habitats. Brine shrimps (family Artemiidae) are found all over the world in saltwater lakes and pools. They have flat, leaf-like appendages with fine bristles, which are waved around to trap food from the water and for swimming. Water fleas (*Daphnia* genus) also belong to this group. They do not have obvious segments and they move in a series of jerks using their antennae.

Classification key	
PHYLUM	Arthropoda
SUB-PHYLUM	Mandibulata
SUPER-CLASS	Crustacea
CLASS	**Branchiopoda (water fleas and brine shrimps)**
SPECIES	800–1000

Amazing facts

- Some species of mussel shrimps emit light to attract **mates**.
- The presence of different **fossils** in layers of rocks (rock strata) can help geologists to date the rocks. Ostracod fossils have been used to locate layers of rock that contain oil.

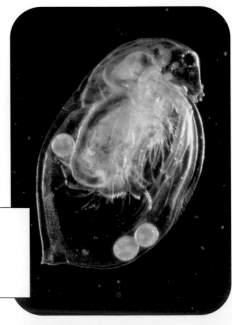

▶ *Daphnia* (a branchiopod) is often found in freshwater **plankton**. All of its body organs are visible through the transparent **carapace**. The eggs develop in a pouch attached to the body.

▶ Fairy shrimps are branchiopods with a long body and no carapace. They swim upside down, using their limbs for feeding as well as **locomotion**.

Cephalocarida

Cephalocarids live in silt or sand on the seabed and feed on dead organic material. They are found up to depths of 1500 metres. They have a head, a **thorax** made up of eight segments, an **abdomen** of eleven segments and a **telson**. The thorax has paddle-like appendages, but there are no appendages on the abdomen. They are very tiny, the biggest being about 3.5 millimetres long.

Classification key

PHYLUM	Arthropoda
SUB-PHYLUM	Mandibulata
SUPER-CLASS	Crustacea
CLASS	**Cephalocarida**
SPECIES	9

Ostracoda

Ostracods are found in marine and freshwater habitats. Most of the body consists of a head with five pairs of appendages. They range in size from 1 millimetre to 3 centimetres in length. They are totally enclosed by their carapace, with only the antennae outside. Most species live at the bottom of seas or lakes, where they crawl around in the mud feeding on decaying matter or other small animals.

Classification key

PHYLUM	Arthropoda
SUB-PHYLUM	Mandibulata
SUPER-CLASS	Crustacea
CLASS	**Ostracoda** **(mussel shrimps)**
FAMILIES	60
SPECIES	6000

▶ The body of an ostracod does not have distinct segments and is totally enclosed by its carapace, which is in two halves.

Centipedes and millipedes

Centipedes and millipedes are land-dwelling arthropods with many legs. Both are divided into two parts: a head and a long, slender body called a trunk. The head has one pair of **antennae** and usually two pairs of biting mouthparts. The eyes, if present, are simple. Typically, there is one pair of legs on each segment of the trunk. The **exoskeleton** does not have a waxy, waterproof layer, so centipedes and millipedes tend to live in damp habitats, such as soil or leaf litter, so that they do not dry up.

Centipedes

Centipedes are found all over the world, from **temperate** to **tropical** regions. Their bodies are long and flattened. There are at least sixteen segments making up the trunk, with one pair of legs on each segment. The long, thread-like antennae are the main sense organs. The **appendages** on the first trunk segment are **adapted** to form a pair of poison claws – hollow structures connected to poison glands. Centipedes are **carnivores**. They hunt at night for slugs, earthworms and soft-bodied insects. They grasp hold of their **prey** using the claws and inject poison into them.

After **mating** with a male, the female lays the **fertilized** eggs, one by one, in soil. The eggs hatch into miniature adults, but have fewer segments. As the young feed and grow, their bodies develop more segments.

Classification key	
PHYLUM	Arthropoda
SUB-PHYLUM	Mandibulata
SUPER-CLASS	Myriapoda
CLASSES	**2 – Chilopoda (centipedes) and Diplopoda (millipedes)**
ORDERS	16
FAMILIES	144
SPECIES	13,700

▼ Centipedes have one pair of legs on each segment of the trunk. They are able to move quickly across the ground.

▲ Scolopendrids are brightly coloured. This species includes some of the largest centipedes in the world, reaching 26 centimetres in length. This one has caught a tarantula.

Millipedes

Millipedes have more cylindrical-shaped bodies. The number of trunk segments varies from one **species** to another: some have 11 segments, while others have more than 100. The trunk segments are fused together in pairs and are called diplosegments. Inside each diplosegment, there are two of everything, so it follows that each has two pairs of legs on the outside. Millipedes are **herbivores** and feed mainly on decaying plants, but they will also eat roots and fruits. When threatened, they roll up into a ball and can produce a foul-smelling liquid to deter their enemies. After mating, the female lays groups of eggs in a nest, which she guards until they hatch.

Amazing facts

- A tropical centipede, *Scolopendra gigantica*, may grow to a length of 260 millimetres.
- Millipedes vary in size, with the smallest being about 2 millimetres long and the longest up to 280 millimetres long.
- The largest millipedes may have up to 750 legs, not a thousand as their name suggests.

▶ Despite having a larger number of legs, millipedes move more slowly than centipedes. The legs appear to move in a wave-like way as the millipede crawls through leaf litter.

Arachnids

Arachnids belong to the sub-phylum Chelicerata, which also includes sea spiders and horseshoe crabs. All chelicerates have a body divided into two parts, a **cephalothorax** and an **abdomen**. There are no **antennae** and the first pair of **appendages** are called **chelicerae**. These are like pincers or fangs and are used in feeding. The second pair of appendages are the **pedipalps**. These may be pincer-like and used to capture **prey**, or covered in tiny hairs that detect changes in temperature, air currents and movement.

Most arachnids live on land. They are nearly all **carnivores** and feed on other arthropods, such as insects. In addition to the chelicerae and pedipalps, there are four pairs of walking legs on the cephalothorax. Arachnids do not have jaws or antennae. Their food is broken up by the chelicerae. Many arachnids have sensory hairs all over the body.

▼ Many spiders spin intricate webs in which they trap their prey.

Spiders

Spiders form one of the largest arachnid orders (see page 48). Large numbers of individuals may be present in a habitat. Spiders differ from other arachnids in having as many as eight eyes, although in a few families there are only two or six. They also have the ability to produce silk, which they use to make webs, trap and wrap their prey, and to make **cocoons**. Spiders are all **predators**, feeding on insects.

Ticks and mites

There are over 30,000 different **species** of ticks and mites. Most species are very small, with mites being about 1 millimetre long and the largest ticks up to 30 millimetres long. There is no clear division between the cephalothorax and the abdomen. Mites live in soil and leaf litter, and some species feed on stored food products such as flour and cheese. Ticks are blood-suckers and all are **parasites**. Their soft, flexible abdomen swells up after a meal of blood.

▲ The typically rounded body of this tick shows no division between the cephalothorax and the abdomen.

Classification key

PHYLUM	Arthropoda
SUB-PHYLUM	Chelicerata (arachnids, sea spiders and horseshoe crabs)
CLASS	**Arachnida**
ORDERS	12 (including spiders, scorpions, harvestmen, ticks and mites)
FAMILIES	450
SPECIES	7500

► The large pedipalps of this imperial scorpion are **adapted** for catching prey such as spiders and small lizards.

Amazing facts

- There may be as many as 160,000 mites in 1 square metre of undisturbed grassland.
- After a meal of blood, the abdomen of a female sheep tick may swell to two or three times its normal size.

Scorpions

Scorpions are found in **tropical** climates. Scorpions have an elongated body and the segmentation of the abdomen is more obvious than in other arachnids. They have large pedipalps with pincers, used for grabbing their prey. The tail forms a sting and can be used to inject poison into prey (see page 53).

Using poisons

Scorpions, pseudoscorpions and most spiders can make poisonous substances, called **venom**. Venom is used to kill **prey** or to paralyse it so that it cannot escape. In some cases, venom is used to warn off a **predator**.

▲ In pseudoscorpions, the venom is made in glands in the pincers of the adapted pedipalps. The inner edge of these pincers is smooth. During courtship, males and females grab hold of each other's pedipalps.

Venom is usually made in special glands in the **cephalothorax** and injected into the prey by fangs. In spiders, the **chelicerae** are **adapted** to form the fangs. In each fang, there is a duct, or passage, down the middle for the venom to pass into the victim as it is bitten. The fangs have a stabbing action, rather than a bite, as the mouthparts of spiders are for sucking rather than biting.

Scorpions have venom glands in the tail at the end of the **abdomen**. The sting is formed in the **telson** and has a sharp point. When threatened, or to calm struggling prey, the scorpion arches its abdomen over its head and uses its sting. Pseudoscorpions look like true scorpions, but they do not have a sting or a tail. Their venom glands are in the claws of the **pedipalps**. As they grasp their prey, the venom is injected into its body.

▲ Wolf spiders are found all over the world, even in Arctic regions.

Amazing facts

○ The Brazilian wandering spider (*Phoneutria fera*) has the largest venom glands of any spider. It can be up to 10 millimetres long and can hold enough venom to kill 225 mice.

○ The tarantella dance got its name because it was believed that by performing this lively Italian dance the venom from the bite of a wolf spider, *Lycosa tarantula*, could be flushed out of the body. The affected person was supposed to dance until they fell down on the ground, sweating and exhausted.

Effects of venom

The venom of most spiders is only harmful to insects as it is too weak to harm larger animals. Only about 30 **species**, including some of the funnel-web spiders, are dangerous to humans. In many species, such as the black widow spider, the venom affects the nerves and causes paralysis. Some forms of venom affect the victim's blood, causing the blood vessels to break down and lead to possible infection.

Arachnids can produce chemical substances, other than poisons. For example, the abdominal glands of whip-scorpions produce harmful acids, which can be squirted at attackers. It is likely that some digestive juices are also injected with the venom. These juices can start the process of breaking down the prey so that it can be taken into the mouth and eaten more easily.

▼ This Goliath bird-eating spider has caught a mouse. These spiders will also eat lizards, frogs and poisonous snakes as well as small birds.

Spiders

Spiders form one of the largest groups of arachnids. All spiders are **carnivores** and many will eat members of their own **species**. Most spiders, with the exception of one group, produce **venom**.

▲ This orb web spider of the genus *Argiope* has fangs that work like pincers. It catches large insects in its orb-shaped web.

Body shape

A spider's body is clearly divided into two parts – the **cephalothorax** and the **abdomen** – with a narrow 'waist' between them. On the head, the **chelicerae** form the poison fangs and the **pedipalps** are sensory structures. There are eight **simple eyes**, arranged in two or three rows. Spiders have four pairs of hollow legs attached to the cephalothorax. The abdomen is covered in soft, stretchy skin. At the tip of the abdomen, there is a group of **spinnerets**, special structures through which silk is produced.

▲ Wolf spiders have excellent eyesight which enables them to hunt at night for their live prey. Male and female wolf spiders often dance together before mating.

Classification key

PHYLUM	Arthropoda
SUB-PHYLUM	Chelicerata
CLASS	Arachnida
ORDER	**Aranae**
FAMILIES	about 100
SPECIES	at least 40,000

▲ The jumping spider has excellent vision. It uses some of its eyes to detect the presence of its prey and the pair in the front to judge distance so that it can pounce on the victim.

Silk

All spiders make strong, stretchy silk. It is used to make webs for trapping **prey**, to wrap up prey so that it cannot escape, and to make **cocoons** to protect developing eggs. Inside the spider's abdomen, there are several silk glands, each one producing a different type of silk. These glands open to the outside through fine tubes in the spinnerets. The silk is produced as a liquid, which hardens as it is pulled into fine threads through the spinnerets by the spider.

Family life

Most spiders live alone and only come together to **mate**. Male spiders are usually smaller than the females, and have to make sure that they are not mistaken for prey and eaten by them. The males find the females by their scent. Among the web-spinner species, the male finds the web of a female and attracts her attention by making the threads vibrate. If he makes the right moves, she will mate with him. A few weeks after mating, the female lays her eggs and makes a silk cocoon around them. In some species, the female stays with the eggs, often carrying the cocoon around with her. When the eggs hatch, the young spiders look like miniature adults but are transparent and have no hairs, spines or claws. They **moult** several times as they grow. Most are independent when they hatch, but the females of some species do guard and feed their young.

Amazing facts

- The silk produced by a spider is stronger than a steel wire of the same thickness.
- The tiniest known spider, *Patu digua*, is 0.37 millimetres long.
- The largest spider, the goliath tarantula, is 90 millimetres long.

Orb web spiders

Webs can vary in shape and size. Some spiders, such as money spiders, build webs that look like little hammocks. Other spiders, such as tarantulas, construct funnel-shaped webs. Orb-shaped webs are circular and are very efficient at trapping flying insects. About 4000 species of spiders spin webs of this type. Most of these belong to the family Araneidae.

Classification key

PHYLUM	Arthropoda
SUB-PHYLUM	Chelicerata
CLASS	Arachnida
ORDER	Aranae
FAMILY	**Araneidae**
SPECIES	4000

Web construction

The first stage is to make a bridge line by carrying a thread of silk between two supports. A slack line is then spun below the bridge line. The spider goes back to the middle of the slack line, fixes a thread and drops down to another support. The thread is pulled taut and a Y-shape is formed. The centre of the Y becomes the centre of the web. More threads are added, radiating out like the spokes of a wheel. The spider moves along the existing threads and trails the new thread behind it. The spider pulls each new thread taut with one of its legs before fixing it to a support. When all the spokes are in place, the spider goes back to the centre and puts in a temporary spiral to keep the spokes in place.

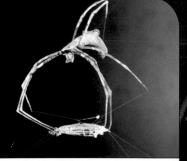

▲ The net-casting spider uses a different method to catch its prey. It hangs upside down, holding the net with four of its legs. When an insect passes, the net is quickly dropped down over the insect, trapping it.

So far, all the threads made have been of non-sticky silk. The spider then moves to an outer edge of the web and begins to lay a final spiral of sticky silk, working inwards. At the centre, the temporary spiral is eaten as the new spiral is laid. Some spiders leave a non-sticky area in the centre of the web and build a platform of silk where they can rest and wait for **prey** to get stuck.

Catching prey

Other spiders spin a non-sticky signal thread, which goes from the centre to the edge of the web. When the web is disturbed, the signal thread is moved and alerts the spider. The spider sits at the edge of the web and waits for the signal thread to vibrate. As soon as the spider feels the vibrations made on the web by a victim, it will move quickly across, keeping to the non-sticky threads. When it reaches its victim, it bites it, injecting **venom** and saliva. It then spins a silk thread to wrap up its meal. Damaged webs are quickly repaired or the spider may construct a new web.

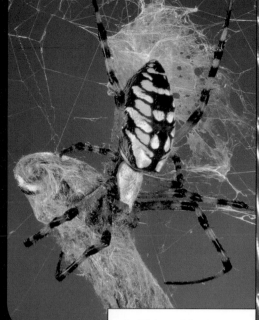

▲ This spider stops its prey escaping by wrapping it in silk.

Amazing facts

- A circular web, about 25 centimetres across, made by a garden spider uses between 20 and 60 metres of silk.
- Orb web spiders taken into space on one of the US Skylab missions built perfect webs, despite being weightless.

◄ The sticky, spiral threads of this wheel-shaped orb web make it very difficult for trapped insects to escape.

Scorpions

Most scorpions are found in **tropical** and sub-tropical regions of the world. Some **species** have **adapted** to life in deserts and dry areas, while others live in the humid conditions of tropical rainforests. Scorpions are **carnivores**, hunting **prey** at night. They hide in burrows, or under stones or logs during the day. Scorpions range in size from 2.5 to 20 centimetres in length.

Body shape

The body of a scorpion is flattened and divided into a **cephalothorax** and an elongated **abdomen**. The upper side of the cephalothorax is protected by the **carapace**. Scorpions have two pairs of eyes – the central pair can see objects and detect movements, while the eyes on either side can only tell the difference between light and darkness. The **pedipalps** are large, with pincers adapted for catching prey. The **chelicerae** also have pincers, which are used to tear up food. The bases of the pedipalps and the first two pairs of walking legs are modified for chewing. Most scorpions feed on insects and spiders, but some catch lizards and small mammals.

▼ Scorpions have complicated courtship behaviour, which ensures that the male is not killed before mating takes place. In many species, males are often killed and eaten by the females after mating.

▲ Female scorpions give birth to live young. They climb on to the mother's back and stay there until their first **moult**.

Classification key

PHYLUM	Arthropoda
SUB-PHYLUM	Chelicerata
CLASS	Arachnida
ORDER	**Scorpiones**
FAMILIES	9
SPECIES	1400

Amazing facts

- Scorpionids may sting their **mates** as part of their complex **mating** ritual.
- Research suggests that scorpions use their chelicerae to kill their victims and only use poison if their prey resists.

The sting

Inside the **telson**, at the end of the abdomen, there are large **venom** glands, which produce deadly poison. On the outside, there is a sharp spine, which is used to pierce the victim and inject the venom. The venom paralyses the victims. Some species, such as *Centruroides noxius*, are found in the USA. These scorpions are dangerous to humans, but will only sting if threatened.

Pseudoscorpions and other look-alikes

Members of several other orders of arachnids look like scorpions, but they differ slightly in structure and their ability to sting. Pseudoscorpions are very small, up to 8 millimetres long, and live in leaf litter, in soil or under stones. They have venom glands in their large pedipalps, but the abdomen is short and there is no sting. Wind scorpions have no poison glands at all. Prey is killed by the chelicerae and held down by the pedipalps while it is being eaten. Whip-scorpions have a long, segmented telson at the end of the abdomen. They produce an acidic liquid, which can be squirted as far as 60 centimetres over an attacker to temporarily blind them.

▶ When a scorpion is about to attack, its claws are held wide apart, open and pointing upwards.

Arthropods under threat

Humans can be affected directly by the activities of arthropods. Many **species** destroy crops or cause serious diseases. On the other hand, there are benefits in the form of food from **crustaceans**, products such as beeswax and honey, the successful pollination of crops and the breakdown of the remains of plants and animals.

Certain arthropod species are under threat of **extinction**. There are about 50 species of crustaceans and 49 species of insects on the Red List of Threatened Species published by the IUCN, also known as the World Conservation Union. These include some crabs, brine shrimps, butterflies and beetles.

Habitat change

The disappearance of land habitats, such as rainforests and natural grasslands, has a major impact on insect and arachnid populations. The impact of the removal of food plants of the insects will spread throughout **food chains**. It is thought that there are thousands of species, particularly insects and other arthropods, that have not been discovered in the rainforests. If the rainforests disappear, these species, together with other **organisms**, may become extinct before anyone discovers them.

▼ Some butterfly species depend on a narrow range of food plants. Destruction of habitats could result in the loss of these plants and the extinction of the butterflies.

Pollution

Pollution involves the addition of chemicals and other waste into natural **ecosystems**. These substances can get into the bodies of arthropods, either directly or through eating infected organisms. There is often an increased quantity of these harmful substances in the animals higher up the food chain. If poisonous chemicals get into the bodies of insects, then these chemicals will be passed on to birds or fish that eat large numbers of the insects. This can happen with poisonous chemicals that are sprayed on crops to kill pests, such as Colorado beetles. The chemicals used to kill harmful insect pests will kill harmless ones as well.

▲ Slash and burn agriculture, where trees are cut down and burnt to clear the land, destroys habitats such as rainforests. Some arthropod species may become extinct before they have been discovered.

Aquatic ecosystems

If harmful chemicals get into water, many arthropod species with **aquatic larvae** become affected. In freshwater ecosystems, insect larvae are at risk and in marine ecosystems pollution can destroy **plankton**. Oil pollution can have a huge impact on marine habitats, covering the surface of the ocean with oil and threatening all plant and animal life in the area. Crustaceans, such as crabs, lobsters and prawns, are harvested in large numbers and eaten by humans. They are becoming scarce in some areas.

Amazing facts

- Tropical rainforests are thought to contain more than half of all the known species of animals, including thousands of species of social insects, such as bees, wasps and ants.
- Studies of the way in which insects fly have contributed to the development of aircraft.

◄ Oil pollution is a serious threat to all marine life.

Protecting arthropods

More research is needed to find and name the large numbers of **species** that inhabit different **ecosystems**. Many arthropods are tiny and escape notice, but they are of great importance in **food chains**. The survival of one species is important for the survival of others in the same habitat.

Protecting habitats

The natural habitat of a species should provide all it needs for survival. By setting up national parks and wildlife reserves, many natural habitats are preserved. It is clear that these parks and reserves do protect larger animals, such as mammals, birds and reptiles. They also preserve arthropods, which, although they are not always as noticeable as the larger animals, are just as important in keeping a balance in the ecosystem.

▼ The spiders and butterflies shown here were collected from the wild for sale to tourists. Laws now protect some rare species from being collected.

▲ The abundance of flowers in gardens, hedgerows and fields provides food for butterflies, such as this peacock butterfly.

Many insects, such as butterflies and moths, depend on specific plants on which to lay their eggs and provide food for their **larvae**. The reduction in the use of weedkillers on roadside verges contributes to the growth of more wild flowers, while the management of woodlands and grasslands encourages the preservation of different habitats. Both these measures increase the range of plants and habitats available to insects. This can be of benefit in the control of pest **organisms** as it provides habitats for their **predators**.

Amazing facts

- The world's largest butterflies, the birdwings, are now protected by law. In 1966, a collector paid £750 for a rare birdwing, *Troides allotei*, from the Solomon Islands.

- Wood ants protect forests because they eat harmful insects. The wood ant was the first insect to be protected by conservation law in Germany in 1880.

Breeding programmes

One way of conserving species is to **breed** them in captivity, so that they can be released back into the wild. **Tropical** butterflies, such as birdwings, are bred in captivity for collectors. This protects the species and stops them being collected in the wild. All over the world, breeding programmes could be used to boost the numbers of many declining species of arthropods in the wild.

Legislation

Laws and agreements can be made between countries to protect wildlife, banning the killing of certain animals or limiting the number that can be caught or killed. There are agreements between countries to protect species of arthropods. For example, it is illegal to collect certain rare butterflies and moths.

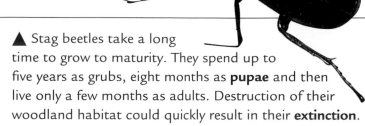

▲ Stag beetles take a long time to grow to maturity. They spend up to five years as grubs, eight months as **pupae** and then live only a few months as adults. Destruction of their woodland habitat could quickly result in their **extinction**.

Classification

Scientists have found and classified about 2 million different types of animals. With so many **species** it is important that they are classified into groups. The groups show how living **organisms** are related by **evolution** and where they belong in the natural world. A scientist identifies an animal by looking at its features, for example, by counting the number of legs or what teeth it has. Animals that share the same **characteristics** belong to the same species. Species with similar characteristics are placed in the same genus. The genera are grouped together in families, families are grouped into orders and orders are grouped into classes. Classes are grouped together in phyla (singular: phylum) and finally, phyla are grouped into kingdoms. Kingdoms are the largest groups and are at the highest level. There are five kingdoms: monerans (bacteria), protists (single-celled organisms), fungi, plants and animals.

Naming an animal

Each species has a unique scientific name, usually known as its Latin name, consisting of two words. The first word is the name of the genus to which the organism belongs and the second is the name of its species. For example, the Latin name of the Peacock butterfly is *Nymphalis io* and that of the Camberwell beauty is *Nymphalis antiopa*. This tells us that these animals are grouped in the same genus but are different species. Many animals are given common names, but this may vary from one part of the world to another. The common shiny woodlouse, *Oniscus asellus*, is also called a 'bibble-bug', a 'gammer-sow', a 'coffin-cutter', a 'pill bug' or a 'cudworm'.

▼ Praying mantids belong to the order Mantodea, characterized by their triangular heads and large eyes. They are the only insects able to turn their heads and look behind them.

Sometimes there are very small differences between individuals that belong to the same species. So there is an extra division called a sub-species. To show that an animal belongs to a sub-species, another name is added on to the end of the Latin name. For example, there are several sub-species of migratory locust, *Locusta migratoria* – *L. migratoria manilensis* (Oriental), *L. migratoria migratoria* (Asian) and *L. migratoroides* (African).

This table shows how a housefly is classified.

Classification	Example: housefly	Features
Kingdom	Animalia	Houseflies belong to the animal kingdom because they have many cells, need to eat food and are formed from a **fertilized** egg.
Phylum	Arthropoda	A housefly is an arthropod because it has a segmented body, an **exoskeleton** and jointed legs.
Sub-phylum	Mandibulata	Animals that possess chewing mouthparts and **antennae** belong to the sub-phylum Mandibulata.
Super-class	Hexapoda	Hexapods have three pairs of legs.
Class	Insecta	Houseflies are insects because they have a **thorax** with three pairs of legs, one or two pairs of wings and an **abdomen**.
Order	Diptera	Dipterans have a pair of front wings and a pair of **halteres** for balancing.
Family	Muscidae	Members of this family are drably coloured, with hairy bodies and mouthparts **adapted** for sucking up liquids.
Genus	*Musca*	A genus is a group of species that are are more closely related to one another than to any other group in the family. *Musca* is the genus for the housefly.
Species	*M. domestica*	A species is a group of individuals that can **interbreed** successfully. *M. domestica* is the complete name for the housefly.

Arthropod evolution

The exact origins of the arthropods are still unknown, but it is assumed that they **evolved** from annelids (worm-like animals). Both groups share some common **characteristics**, such as the presence of segmented bodies, but arthropods developed a firm **exoskeleton**.

▲ In addition to their keen eyesight, which enables them to judge distances, jumping spiders have sturdy front legs that can hold **prey** firmly when they land on their victims.

Peripatus – the missing link?

In the search for a definite link between annelids and arthropods, the characteristics of a **primitive** arthropod called *Peripatus* (the velvet worm) were investigated. *Peripatus* has a segmented, worm-like body covered in dry skin, about 20 pairs of short legs and a head with **antennae** and **mandibles**. It looks like a relative of a modern centipede. **Fossils** of an animal very similar to *Peripatus* had been discovered in rocks dating back to a time before the **evolution** of centipedes, more than 500 million years ago. However, more recent fossil evidence, together with more details of the life cycle and structure of *Peripatus*, showed that the ancestors of the velvet worm had no direct links with annelids.

Fossil evidence

There is some evidence to suggest that fossil trilobites were the ancestors of arthropods. Trilobites, known to exist 570 million years ago, have features in common with arthropods, particularly **crustaceans**. The bodies of trilobites were divided into three parts, they had antennae and jointed limbs and **larval** stages like crustaceans.

◄ Tarantulas are mygalomorph spiders (their fangs strike downwards, instead of closing sideways like pincers). They are considered to have evolved before other groups of spiders.

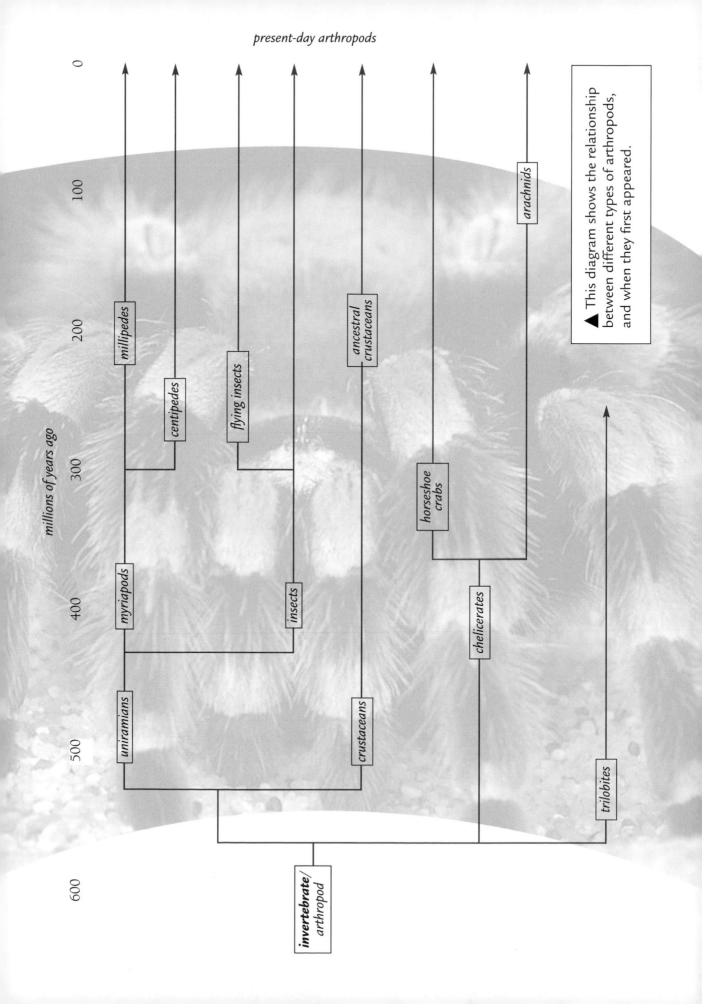

present-day arthropods

millions of years ago

0

100

200

300

400

500

600

millipedes

centipedes

flying insects

ancestral crustaceans

arachnids

myriapods

insects

horseshoe crabs

chelicerates

uniramians

crustaceans

trilobites

invertebrate/arthropod

▲ This diagram shows the relationship between different types of arthropods, and when they first appeared.

Glossary

abdomen rear part of an arthropod's body behind the thorax

adapt change in order to cope with the environment

air current movement of air

antenna (plural: **antennae**) feeler on an arthropod's head, used to smell, touch and taste

appendage projection, such as a leg, from the body

aquatic living in water

breed mate and produce young

camouflage colouring that blends with the background, making an animal difficult to see

carapace covering over the cephalothorax in crustaceans and arachnids

carnivore animal that eats other animals

caste group of insects that carries out a particular role in a colony

cephalothorax front part of the body of some arthropods, formed from the head and thorax

characteristic feature or quality of an animal, for example having wings or antennae

chelicera (plural: **chelicerae**) first pair of appendages in an arachnid

chrysalis pupal stage in the life cycle of a butterfly or moth

cocoon case made to contain eggs for spiders; or a pupal case for insects

colony group of organisms, such as bees, that live together

compound eye arthropod eye made up of a large number of tiny lenses

crustacean arthropod that has antennae, eyes on stalks and a shield-like covering over the head and thorax

cuticle tough substance that forms the exoskeleton of an arthropod

ecosystem the interaction between living organisms and the environment in which they live

evolution slow process of change in living organisms so that they can adapt to their environment

evolve change very slowly over a long period of time

exoskeleton skeleton made of a tough material on the outside of an animal's body

extinct no longer in existence, permanently disappeared

fertilize coming together of an egg (from a female) and sperm (from a male) to form a new individual

food chain organisms that depend on each other for food

fossil remains, trace or impression of ancient life preserved in rock

gill part of the body that an aquatic animal uses to collect oxygen from water, in order to breathe

halteres modified hind wings of flies, used as balancing organs

herbivore animal that eats plants

hermaphrodite organism that has both male and female sex organs

interbreed mate with another animal of the same species

invertebrate animal without a backbone

larva (plural: **larvae**) young animal that looks different from the adult and changes shape as it develops; second stage of arthropod life cycle

locomotion movement from one place to another

mandibles jaws of an arthropod, especially insects

mate (noun) reproduction partner of the opposite sex

mate (verb) ability of male to fertilize the eggs of a female of the same species

membrane thin sheet of body tissue

metamorphosis change in body shape from larva to adult

migrate journey to a different area for part of the life cycle

moult shed the exoskeleton to allow for growth

nectar sweet liquid produced by plants on which butterflies and bees feed

nymph larva of an insect that undergoes incomplete metamorphosis

organic material from plants or animals

organism any living thing

parasite animal that lives on or in another animal and causes it harm

pedipalps second pair of appendages of an arachnid

plankton tiny plants and animals that live in water

pores tiny openings in the surface of skin

predator animal that hunts other animals

prey animal that is killed and eaten by a predator

primitive at an early stage of evolution or development, for example scorpions are considered to be more primitive than spiders

proboscis long, thin structure used by butterflies and moths to suck up nectar

pupa third stage in the life cycle of an insect that goes through complete metamorphosis

regurgitate bring food back into the mouth

respiration the breathing in of oxygen and the breathing out of carbon dioxide

rostrum in insects, set of mouthparts that look like a beak; or the front part of the carapace in crustaceans

serrated saw-like

simple eye eye with a single lens

skeleton framework of rigid material giving support to the body either inside or outside

species group of individuals that share many characteristics and which can interbreed to produce offspring

spinneret organ on the abdomen of a spider through which silk is drawn

spiracles openings in the exoskeleton of the thorax and abdomen that allow an insect to breathe

sterile unable to produce offspring

telson tail fan at the end of the abdomen of a crustacean

temperate mild climate

thorax middle part of the body of an arthropod

trachea (plural: **tracheae**) tube taking air into an animal's body

tropical relating to the hot regions of the world between the tropic of Cancer and the tropic of Capricorn

tropics hot regions of the world between the tropic of Cancer and the tropic of Capricorn

venom poison

vertebrate animal that has a backbone

zooplankton tiny animals that form part of the plankton

Further information

BOOKS TO READ

Burton, Maurice and Peter, *The Encyclopedia of Insects and Invertebrates* (Little Brown, 2003)

Burnie, David (ed.), *Animal: the Definitive Visual Guide to the World's Wildlife* (Dorling Kindersley, 2001)

Chinery, Michael, *Garden Creepy-Crawlies* (Whittet Books, 1986)

Greenaway, Theresa, *The Secret World of Crabs* (Raintree, 2003)

Preston-Mafham, Ken, *The Secret World of Butterflies and Moths* (Raintree, 2000)

USEFUL WEBSITES

http://animaldiversity.ummz.umich.edu
Website of the Museum of Zoology, University of Michigan. This website has detailed information on all animal groups.

http://www.bbc.co.uk/nature
Find information on all kinds of animals from invertebrates to mammals.

http://www.monarchwatch.org/biology
This site contains lots of information on the Monarch butterfly.

Disclaimer
All the Internet addresses (URLs) given in this book were valid at the time of going to press. However, due to the dynamic nature of the Internet, some addresses may have changed, or sites may have changed or ceased to exist since publication. While the author, the packager and Publishers regret any inconvenience this may cause readers, no responsibility for any such changes can be accepted by either the author, the packager or the Publishers.

Index